Perceiving Courage

Susan Kleinberg

Published in the United States by XPLR Productions, LLC.
The text of this work is comprised of the audio conversations by Ms. Kleinberg and photographs taken or
chosen by her for her 2001 Venice Biennale installation
"FEAR NOT/NON TEMERE"

Library of Congress Cataloging-in-Publication Data
Names: Kleinberg, Susan 1949– author.
Title: PERCEIVING COURAGE / Susan Kleinberg
Description: First edition. | New York: XPLR Productions,
LLC, [2020].
Identifiers: Library of Congress Control Number:
2020925417
ISBN 978-0-578-85024-5

ISBN 978-0-578-85024-5

susankleinberg.com

Cover design: Susan Kleinberg

Cover photograph: "KAIROS 1.1" from KAIROS
installation, Palazzo Fortuny, Venice. 2015.
(c) 2015 by Susan Kleinberg.

Kairos is the Greek word for the moment in time
in which something happens.

CONTENTS

INTRODUCTION

This is a book as much about the will to live as it is about courage. Such curious phenomena – phenomena that we all question at some point; profoundly, daily, suddenly, unexpectedly.

I began this investigation with no thesis, nothing to prove, no ax to grind. I walked down a small road with an extremely low-rent tape recorder to a fire department. Adrenaline pumping, I approached one of the firemen, who was outside fiddling with the hoses on his truck. I asked him if he would talk with me about what he thought courage was.

He was on his lunch break and all he had was a decrepit looking tuna sandwich. So I lucked out as a diversion. We started talking, soon joined by his colleagues. The question of courage proved to be a wedge in: beyond the social, the defended, the predictable – a key to thoughts unacknowledged, certainly unexpressed. I spent the afternoon at the firehouse, primarily listening. I learned a great deal: How one must reveal themselves in order to be revealed to; how to pay attention; how what happens, what is said and done, exists in a space all its own -- neither one person or the other, of its moment, unrepeatable, unreproducible, ephemeral, a gift, an effort, a pain, a catalyst, a treasure.

I thought, "How can this phenomena of what people find, become, in extreme circumstances, be they dramatic or subtle, be transferred to others, to a general knowledge, without the horror of having to endure the experience? How is it that so much good, such positive, emerges at the far edge of our capacity and is utterly lost in the venal of daily life?

Is there a way to put this forward? Where do the challenges lie? Can it contribute? Can its entirely fresh ground communicate through the preconception of such a battle-worn concept, "courage."

At the end of my afternoon with the firemen something had happened, to them, to me. My tape recorder had been rendered invisible.

This was essential. The process would never work if it were self-conscious. This made for infinite hours of editing, but surely worth it.

I began photographing each person with whom I spoke, as a record for myself. They were not portraits, they were glimpses, photographed fast, unposed, informally. They became portraits, with the conversations, portraits of possibility, of each individual, of their similarities and differences, where they'd landed on this earth, what they saw, how they saw.

From the firemen, I continued on, speaking with the publicly known and unknown. In many ways no one was more interesting than the next – the electrician on a back street, General Norman Schwarzkopf in his office in Florida.

The electrician was surrounded by the tools of his trade and the inquiries of his community who valued his considerations. General Schwarzkopf was surrounded by photographs of dogs, many with birds in their mouths, and photographs with children. Not one photograph of anything remotely military. And his phone rang with the same inquiries as the electrician's customers.

What happened between each of us was different and the same. I never knew what I would hear. The line between the dramatic and the prosaic became blurry, the material of courage porous and immune to definition.

My interest was always the question.

For myself, I tend to integrate my experience obliquely. I never quite know from where things arrive and make art to see how they form. I didn't set out to understand or make order of my own experiences or emotions, but I had some grounds. Pretty well a Pandora's box full: A broken body drawn and quartered by a water-skiing accident in the shark-infested sea off Panama; an attack of the impossibility to breath, on an island down a river in Belize; a rare form of cancer, causing uncertainty to be as much a component of each day as the sun and the moon, complicated by responses of the heart. Its return ten years later, its return again. Surviving – why?

The acuteness of the essential moment, fading back to life and its pains, stresses and difficulties. At first thrilled to feel their normalcy, then to find oneself again available to be preyed upon by the attacks on one's soul, by the emotions of interchange – the challenge of how to stay positive, knowing a bit too much. The world, as it turns unjustly, brokenly, why fight? What is this will to live? What is couage? Where do you place yourself within it?

This book tracks this exploration through many conversations:

Congressman John Lewis, astronaut Sally Ride, former Secretary of State Madeleine Albright, former President Bill Clinton, author Gore Vidal, Dr. Holly Andersen, domestic worker Santa Isaacs … their challenges, their fears, my fears, their terrors, their doubt, where they find beauty, value, where they don't.

It takes the form of a prologue of my experience, my journey to each person, often an extremely interesting quest; telling these inside stories, at the beginning of the chapters, as a thread to weave the book together. For example, how does a New York artist in entirely too much black, move through the echelons of bishops in scarlet to attempt to speak to the Pope? She gets frisked by guards in uniforms designed by Michelangelo, sits in back of the Queen of Spain while watching the faces of 40 princes of the Church at the Mass in which they are made Cardinals pass through the immensity of their relationship to this wedding, as they are given their rings by the Pope, an ancient man leaning on his staff, speaking at the edge of language. I was invited to record this mass, up close. No one interviews the Pope.

The book is propelled from conversation to conversation, each reflecting, commenting, challenging the next: The gondolieri in Venice, as they know of nature. Astronaut Sally Ride and the normalcy, to her, of riding a rocket past the moon, her awe and admiration at the magnitude of the capacity and the difficulty of the actions of civil rights pioneer Rosa Parks. Former President Bill Clinton, at the height of his impeachment hearings, tapping the spoon to his saucer, continually, unthinkingly, a metronome as he talked.

Dr. Holly Andersen questioning what she can really do to intervene in life-threatening situations, emphasic in her committment to try. Chuck Close, in his perseverance, his joke, "Do you know why New Yorkers are so depressed? Because the light at the end of the tunnel is New Jersey." His thought that, no matter how impossible it seems at the moment, you will be happy again. Gore Vidal showing me his miraculous garden, declaring there is no such thing as courage. It is an adjective.

In contrast to Vidal, Cong. John Lewis, a living embodiment of courage by any definition. Domestic worker Santa Isaacs sees her every day as courageous, she aches, but then she goes shopping.

These conversations have been presented as a visual-audio art installation, from the Venice Biennale to MoMA PS1 to the Museum of Fine Arts in Buenos Aires, the Foundation Sandretto Re Rebaudengo in Turin, Italy...

My purpose is to create a dialogue with the reader, as they read on from one to the next in joy, in confusion, in doubt, in hope, to locate themselves.

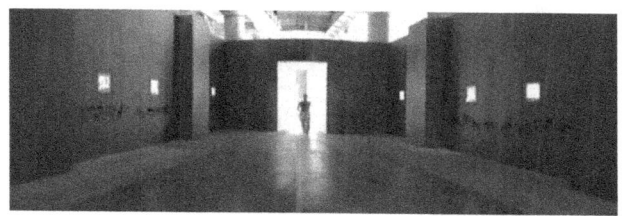

"Fear Not" Installation, Arsenale, Venice Biennale 2001

Photo Credit: Les Guthman

Congressman John Lewis

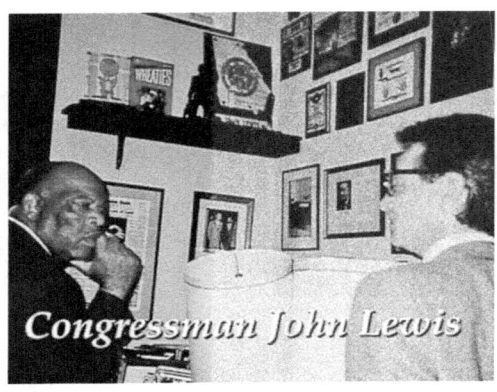

Congressman John Lewis

Congressman John Lewis' office was an exceptional ar-
chive of an exceptional life. To walk down the vast reverber-
ating halls of Congress, thinking of his marches: Crossing the
Pettus Bridge in Selma, leading the Freedom Riders in their
journey through the Deep South, accompanying Martin Luther
King in Atlanta, does not begin to prepare you for the jolt of
entering this modest man's modest office with the artifacts and
images of a memorable life.

It was crammed full. Bales of cotton unlabeled, images of
Medgar Evers, Bobby Kennedy, photographs of burning cars
you've definitely seen before, exquisite images of poor Southern families, a Wheaties box that says, "Breakfast of Champi-
ons," signed with thanks from a president; a young John Lewis
in a coat and tie feeding chickens.

Congressman Lewis entered in his immaculae coat and
tie, but what I thought was, here is a man dressed in his integrity. He had an amazing voice – deep and slow, beyond slow,
deep with material. His words were thoughtful and emphatic,
all part of a cadence, an atmosphere he created quite uncon-
sciously.

He told stories you know he had been asked to tell many times, but they were clearly fresh – I think because he was concerned for you, there, whoever you were, hearing them.

As we talked, the incredibly jarring buzzer calling members of Congress to vote kept ringing over and over. Congressman Lewis was not in the least bit disturbed. It was just trifling punctuation – somehow appropriate even though it coud have awakened the dead at Antietam.

At a certain point he asked if I'd mind if he went to vote, promising to return, which he did, without missing a word.

I asked, "What do you think courage is?"

"Courage is the ability to sail against the wind. It's the ability to move on with faith, with hope; to stand up and fight when it's not easy. Courage is the ability to put your body on the line for a great cause. It's the willingness to face fear and move on in spite of the fear. It is the ability to face dangers, even the possibility of death itself, without turning back, or giving up, or giving in, or giving out.

"During my life I've seen many people face unbelievable odds. We were told during the Freedom Ride in May 1961 that we would never make it from Selma to Birmingham, or from Birmingham to Montgomery, or from Montgomery to Jackson, Mississippi. We were met by angry mobs. We were beaten, left lying bloody and unconscious, but we didn't give up. We were arrested, jailed, sent to the state penitentiary; but we didn't give up.

"On the march from Selma to Montgomery, we were met by a group of state troopers. I was hit in the head by a state trooper with a nightstick and had a concussion. I thought I was going to die. I thought I saw death that day. Sometimes I feel like saying I stared death down. I really thought it was the last protest for me, but I didn't give up. In spite of the violence, having the concussion, being jailed 40 times, I still believed there comes a time when you must be willing to give a cause, a movement, all you have. And that's what I've tried to do for more than 40 years."

"What do you draw from for that capacity?"

"You come to a point when you've been jailed, had a lighted cigarette put out in your hair, down your back, when you lose all sense of fear. You say, "What else can you do to me? You can kill me, but you're not going to stop me from doing what I believe to be right.

"On the march from Selma to Montgomery, it was peaceful, orderly, non-violent. On that day I thought we were going to be arrested, go to jail. I didn't have any idea we were going to be attacked. But I think what happened that day gave me a greater resolve to do what I can for the rest of my life. To stand up and fight for what is right, makes no different the cause, makes no difference what happens, you just have to do it.

"Sometimes I think an act of courage means putting yourself in the way. You don't know how it's going to come out, you don't know what the results are going to be, but you have to go, you have to put yourself in the way, be willing to offer your very being, your very body, as a living witness to the truth.

"Sometimes I think, in our society today, that we're just too quiet. And maybe we need inspiration. We need to be moved to that point where once again we're ready to make a little noise, to push a little, to agitate a little."

"Do you think when you come to a point that's so extreme, it changes you forever?"

Congressman Lewis continued, "Whether it's a march across the Pettus Bridge in Selma, whether it's the Freedom Rides in Montgomery, when you face death and in a sense get to a point where you cannot turn back, you cannot turn around, you must go on. It changes you.

"Those of us who went on the Freedom Rides didn't know whether we were going to return or not. There were 13 of us on the original ride, seven whites and six blacks. To board a

Greyhound Bus in Washington, D.C. and travel through the South in an interracial fashion was very, very dangerous. But we had to do it. We had to do it to make real the laws of this land.

"I knew my life would never, ever be the same the moment I was arrested for the first time 40 years ago. Because people had used arrest, jail, lynchings, to sort of frighten people into submission. We used to sing a little song, 'We ain't scared of your jails, you never can jail us all.' I think all of that helped change and mold me, and so many others, to come to that point where you love an idea so much, you love a cause, you love your country and what your country stands for so much, that you come to a point you're willing to die for it."

Sally Ride
Astronaut

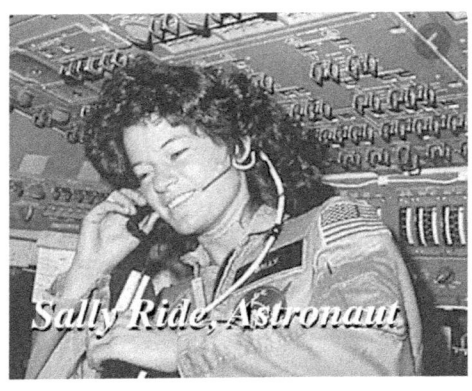

I was on my way to meet an astronaut. When I was a child in Arizona, I wrote to the president volunteering. I got a very nice letter back saying they weren't accepting little girls into the astronaut program just now, but please keep them in mind – and I have. Had I not been utterly inept at math, severely near-sighted and claustrophobic, I would surely have pursued it. Still, I would go in a minute.

Sally Ride taught at the University of California San Diego. She generously agreed to see me before her first astrophysics class of the morning. I was organizing this from Los Angeles, so it meant getting up with the sun -- which was perfect. I was having an entirely private, even hoarded, artist-parallel experience.

I got into the car in the dark, excited and not entirely sure what would emerge with the dawn. Of course, what emerged was not the edge of the universe or the perspective of infinite scale of our pin prick world, but the freeway was slick and starry and came to have a rosy glow somewhere near two breast-like nuclear reactors close to a gold-domed semi-Arabic self-realization center.

Dr. Ride had two parking spaces, so I parked in the one that said, "Accelerator." It was dewy early morning, with a dense smell of the sea – just as I imagined Cape Canaveral. In the car, I ran through an equipment check, zipped up my suit and stepped out.

Sally Ride had a prototypical academic's office in an entirely predictable academic building – until you looked again. The innocuous dentist-office photographs and prints were real. It was our history of exploration, of possibility, of accomplishment against enormous odds – potent images of scientific force and engineered nature.

A carton of slightly stale doughnuts rested on a counter. No aficionado of "Apollo 13" could miss those doughnuts or the Mission Control coffee with packets of creamer sure to remain preserved on Mars.

A high priority of Dr. Ride was science programming for young women. The many students milling around were affable in a kind of nonchalant intense way.

There were several urgent messages for Dr. Ride from NASA tucked under a Diet Coke on the desk where I waited. I looked around a corner to find a peeling sticker, "Ride Sally Ride."

I began our conversation in my own reverie, "I can only imagine that the moment of stepping into the shuttle must have been quite a moment, even after all the training."

She answered, "Yes it was, although the whole sequence of events that you go through on launch morning are a bit of a blur. You get up at three in the morning and then there are a set of things that you do, all of them focused towards getting into the shuttle and launching. And it's kind of a big deal, so you really have to focus on it and focus on the sequence of events and making sure that everything's done that's supposed to be done.

"I didn't really have much time, didn't really notice, stepping into the shuttle, that I had just stepped into the shuttle. I'd stepped into the shuttle many times before, so it really wasn't a defining moment or anything like that. It was just one part of a sequence of things that morning."

She considered, "It's a bit of a blur. Probably the part that I enjoyed most was looking back at the earth. The view of earth and the experience of being in space, being weightless and circling the world, was a spectacular feeling."

I asked how she felt courage entered into this. She answered, "I think maybe courage is being willing to do things that you should do and that you have to do when it's not the easiest thing in the world. I don't know whether being an astronaut falls into that category or not. I would think of a fire fighter or police officer as a much more courageous person than an astronaut. I mean, an astronaut has got a fun job, and has an unbelievable opportunity and really, rather than being courageous in going up in space, you're just kind of balancing this wonderful opportunity versus the risk, and making some decision of whether the risk is acceptable for you.

"All the astronauts have a pretty good appreciation for the risk. That was true before the Challenger accident and it's been true since the Challenger accident. I think most of us were surprised at the cause of the problem, but I don't think that many of us were surprised that an accident like that happened. In fact, what's maybe more surprising is that another accident hasn't happened, because if you look at the track record of all rockets, even the ones that have been used 100, 150 times, even after they've been successful 50, 60, 70 times, something goes wrong. The space shuttle right now has by far the highest success ratio of any launch vehicle. Astronauts are pretty well aware that a launch vehicle, a very good launch vehicle, tends to be successful 96-97 percent of the time. That means if you launch a hundred times, three times are not gonna be good days

"In the simulators, bad things happen and they happen on Monday, Tuesday, Wednesday, Thursday and Friday. So, it just does not, you know, it does not take a rocket scientist to appreciate that all of these are credible failures. They all could happen. Last month, we died in the simulator. Fortunately, it was a simulator. But you really get a very good chance to see the reality of what could happen and what could go wrong."

I wondered if she felt she was going into the unknown at any point.

"I didn't really feel like I was going into the unknown. I mean it was enough that I was going into space. There had been Mercury flights and Gemini flights, Apollo flights, there had been a fair number of people up in space before me, so it's not like I was the first person ever into space, and that's my definition of going into the unknown. Allan Shepard went into the unknown. The space shuttle astronauts don't really go into the unknown, but they have an absolutely extraordinary experience."

I continued, "If you had a chance to go beyond, to go into the unknown, would you jump at it?"

Immediately she answered, "Oh, I'd love to go Mars! I'd do that in a second."

I asked whom she might consider courageous through history.

Thinking a minute, she surprisingly said, "I'd probably say Rosa Parks. If you think about it, that takes more courage than most of us have ever been able to muster."

"Yes."

"A different sort of courage than Allan Shepard stepping into a capsule on top of a rocket. But maybe something that was much more difficult to do, given the circumstances. And then, of course, I'd pick Allan Shepard, in a field closer to my own."

"You did mention they canceled the flight that you were going on after the Challenger. Would you have gone?"

"Yeah, I would of."

The disaster wouldn't have made you ...

 "No."

"... bag it?"

"No, uh-uh."

Santa Issacs
Domestic Worker

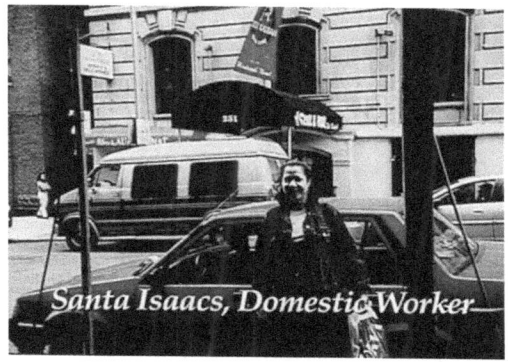

Santa Isaacs is a hero to me.

"To me, courage means like I'm doing everything, you know, by myself. You know, I wake up, I go to work, work hard, very hard. Sometimes when I get home, I have pain everywhere on my body. But I said, 'Well, I had to do it' because, you know, I don't have nobody to pay my bills! You know, but I'm happy, because when I have pain, then I think about later what I'm going to get. Oh the pain, all the pain gone!"

Gore Vidal
Author

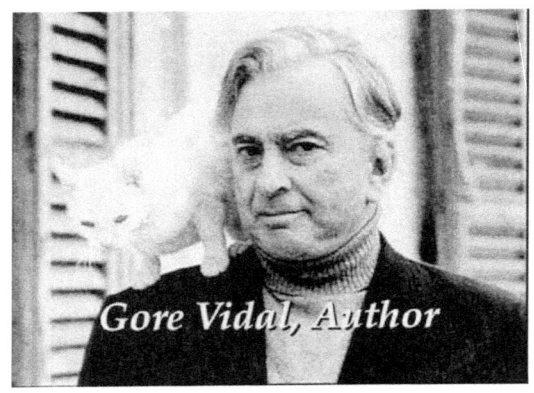

Gore Vidal, Author

Gore Vidal inspired fear at its best. One wrong word might decimate you.

I met Gore Vidal at a party on the bank of the Venetian Lagoon facing out to the open sea. My contact lens had just fallen down the toilet. I'd been installing a sculpture, which this party was marginally celebrating, wet head to toe with the effluence of Venice and pretty well reduced to the mono-syllabic. Not the best position from which to meet one of the major wits of our time. I was hungry, most were talking. Gore was hungry and knew these conversations by heart. We ate everything, doing the fashion courage review as the parade of well-dressed imagination and lack thereof filtered by. Happily nasty. As we left, I tucked the phone number he'd surprisingly offered into my limp but fashionable shoe and forgot it.

In the following months, I was working in Rome and was offered the chance to do a project at a ceramics factory on the Amalfi Coast. In spite of the fact that I knew less than nothing about ceramics and had never wanted to, I said "yes The factory was perched over the sea in an old monastery. Picasso, etc., had all worked there at some point. I had a friend in Naples to stay with and commuted down the coast during the week.

This is not so easy, as it necessitates negotiating the Neo-politan train station, which is not stocked with large quantities of talismans of protection for no reason.

The staple products of this factory were sad-eyed madon-nas, every color, every gesture, every down-cast glance. When an artist came to work they gave the madonnas a break and came to watch the work progress from about six inches away. A rotating group of five through ten hovered at this distance all day every day. They were curious, often outraged, gener-ous, talented and difficult to communicate with owing to the rich southern dialect they spoke, which unfortunately I couldn't understand. About eleven-thirty one morning, I'd had it. Fairly desperate, I searched my address book, "Do I know anyone around here who doesn't paint madonnas?"

I called Gore in Ravello, an immaculate hillside town not far away. I asked if he would talk with me, as I was preparing a piece about courage. He said no.

I backtracked as fast as possible and still got invited to lunch.

It was real/mythic.

One enters Ravello through an arch: A curved architrave into an altered world. Gore lived at its edge in the midst of an exquisite garden. He was Papal and less well than years previ-ous. We sat in chairs from the set of Ben Hur, which he wrote, and got drunk. I cared considerably less if he talked with me and the tape recorder, which somehow seemed to be happen-ing, but I certainly cared to be listening.

As I did with everyone, I asked what he thought courage was. He answered, "Well, to do something you regard as vir-tuous for its own sake over the objections of public opinion, family, friends, your own self-interest, that is courage. And it's a constant in human affairs. It's not very common, very few people put themselves at risk for anything.

"I would give the example of my grandfather, Senator Thomas Pryor Gore, inventor of Oklahoma, and his cousin, Albert Gore, Sr., senator from Tennessee and father of President Clintron's vice president.

"The two senator Gores had usual political careers, which are filled with everything from courage to cowardice. But in the big things, Senator T.P. Gore, my grandfather, in 1917, was against America's entry into World War I. His constituents in Oklahoma were gung-ho for war. They didn't really understand much about war and it was the Chamber of Commerce, which felt they'd make money out of it. And there was Sen. Gore saying, 'No, I'm against Mr. Wilson's war and I shall vote against it.' So the Chamber of Commerce of Oklahoma City sent him a telegram saying if you don't vote in favor of our entering the war on the side of the Allies you will be an ex-senator.

"My grandfather sent the Chamber of Commerce a telegram saying, 'How many members of the Chamber are of Draft age?' And three years later, he was an ex-senator. They defeated him. He came back, however, a few years later.

"Comes the Vietnam War, Senator Albert Gore Sr. of Tennessee, I think alone of the Southern delegation - Southern senators usually like wars - was against the Vietnam War, practically alone in the Senate. And the grandees of Tennessee said, 'Unless you support the Vietnam War you will be an ex-senator.' He came out against the war and was duly defeated. And he never came back.

"So there are two examples of courage in the same family. I can't say that I see any other members of the family demonstrating courage of that sort."

I hazarded the question of who in history he would consider courageous.

He looked out over the Tyrrhenian Sea with an instruction or two to a passing gardener. "There's no one courageous on earth. There's never been anyone who was born courageous or maintained a courageous persona.

"It's an adjective, there are only courageous acts. There are no courageous people.

"Some people do more courageous acts than others, but nobody does very many. Otherwise they would not have had careers and we wouldn't be talking about them, because we would never have heard of them. It's those who compromise who rise to high office."

We had been talking about Buddhism earlier, so I asked about this less ego-driven perspective.

He answered, "Well, you're talking about a totally different mindset. However, the Buddha who opts for Sunyata, the "Shining Nothingness" of the last incarnation, I suspect that takes a bit of courage.

To die and know you're forever dead, and not to be reincarnated, that must have given Gautama a slight twinge."

There were several clear, severe, inward-looking Buddhas in the living room. I continued, "Do you think it's more difficult today in our society than in the past?"

In perfect Vidal, he answered, "I think it's probably impossible. We are nothing but administrative numbers, there are no individuals now. Everybody is more or less a reflection of everyone else, which in turn is a reflection of a kind of crude image which is drawn for us by television and popular opinion, which is usually cretinous and cowardly and conformist.

Anyone really courageous would probably be stoned to death in an hour."

Madeleine Albright
Former Secretary of State and U.N. Ambassador

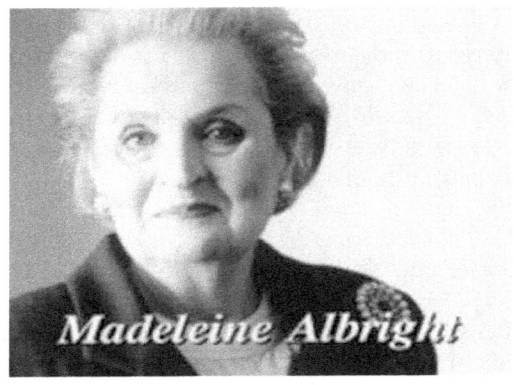

I never expected my prevailing impression of Madeleine Albright to be generosity. She is absolutely present in the moment, fresh, clear, concerned and engaged, like a very young person.

The walls of her office are filled with cartoons of political life, and there is an abundance of good candy, which she offers, and eats.

I asked her, "What do you think courage is?"

"Some of it has to do with physical courage, because I think a lot of things happen when people are forced into physical situations that are very difficult for them, not just with guns, but isolation and torture, which affect your whole mental state.

"Being able to stand up for what you believe in through thick and thin, and sometimes it can also be when things are too good and you forget what your principals are, because you're being lauded, or talked out of what it is you believe for pragmatic reasons.

"So courage is keeping your lodestar and being able to get through everything in order to live up to whatever principles you have."

"Interesting that it can be involved with things being too good..."

She continued, "Take Vaclav Havel, someone who'd been in prison and knew how to operate very well in terrible conditions. Then he becomes president of the Czech Republic and everybody is praising him – he stands on balconies and is lauded by the world. It's very tempting to give up on the things you believe in when you all of a sudden feel you've accomplished something. Havel hasn't given up. So I feel there's courage in sticking with what you're doing even when you're being lionized."

I asked, "What do you think people draw on for courage?"

"Of course you never really know. But some of it has to do with pure inner strength, a belief in not just yourself, but a higher goal, whether it's in God or some deep belief you have. A lot happens – you don't know you have the courage.

"As I was thinking about what I was going to say to you, I've found some of the most courageous people ordinary people you've never heard of. I was in Uganda, where two doctors set up a hospital to do HIV-AIDS, and basically no one knew. So it's not a question of limelight. It's being called upon to do more than you ever thought you would be called upon to do.

"Or the women in Rwanda who had been raped and produced children who were the wrong ethnic group. These people existed in the most unbelievably horrendous conditions. I don't know what made them go on. When you think about watching your child being hacked to death, or being raped and having a child that everyone hated...

"I've been talking with someone who has just come back from camps in Pakistan, who says that 100,000 people are going to starve no matter what happens. How do you move on?

Or in Kosovo, I talked to people who had watched their families being killed and decided to go on. For me it's these people, who just slug it out."

"What do you draw on for your own courage?"

"What I was surprised about myself was that I was not physically afraid. That surprised me. What I drew on was the unbelievable honor of being in the job in the first place. I thought I had to live up to everything that was expected of me, and more. It's not a conscious thing, I don't think of myself as particularly courageous. But whatever it was that I did, there's an instinct that takes over and you pray that your instincts are right. Sometimes you make mistakes, but you have to call upon what's inside you, how you've been raised and what you think are the right things.

"The hardest part is to keep going, even if you're being criticized, which in my case was minor in comparison to people who were arrested or anything like that, huge physical discomfort, being alone, not knowing if people know what's happening to you.

"There are so many different levels of things that happen to people. You wonder where your instincts come from. In my case, I decided that I myself was not important, that it was whatever it was that I was doing that was important. But I was surprised that I was not physically afraid – granted I was pretty well protected. But I had rocks thrown at me and was flying in helicopters with guns out – stuff like that. In some ways you're not there, you're kind of looking at yourself doing things."

"Did you ever think you would be in these kind of circumstances?"

"Never, never. So it's kind of like watching a movie and afterwards you think, "That really happened.""

I continued, "In my case, I think there's a certain level of unreality about these extreme circumstances."

"Yes, right. But I honestly don't know how I would react to being totally deprived of everything. I think about these Afghan women. I met with a group of Afghan women in Peshawar. A lot of them were quite young. They had watched their mothers or sisters being raped – and this was one of the better refugee camps. They worried about what they had left behind. They weren't able to bathe or talk to anybody.

"I happen to believe that we're all actually the same. I traveled 1,038,000 miles as Secretary of State and I've been to about 120 countries. I've met with ordinary people and royalty. You peel all that off and people are all the same.

"Do you think there is a difference between public courage and personal courage?"

"Probably, but I don't know how to describe it. There's something that happens when you're in public, 'I have to pull myself together because everyone is watching.' So that adrenaline kicks in. That's one kind of adrenaline, I can't talk about deprivation, being all alone, but I'm sure there's another kind of adrenaline that kicks in that keeps you going. Clearly, there's an extra something that happens to you when you have to perform.

I don't know if it's chemical, emotional or spiritual, but something does happen. It's the thing you hear about – people picking up refrigerators, something they couldn't do. Something like that happens when you're faced with a terrible situation. Some people fold, and some are able to call on that extra something."

"Is it the same when you face great sadness in your personal life, illness, upset, challenge with people you love? I think it's quite the same."

Secretary Albright paused, "I've gone through personal pain and maybe because I've gone through that, I was better about the other things. There's something cumulative that happens, if you've survived one horrible thing, then you think,

'Well, nothing can be like that.' And you go on. Some people can deal with illness and death better. And it doesn't mean that they're not courageous in other aspects. It subdivides into things. I was pretty good about physical danger, but I'm not sure I'm good about being sick."

I asked, "Do you think that your experience in the positions you've held has affected your concept of courage?"

"Sure. It's put me in touch with people who I would never have known or seen. I'm always asked who are the most extraordinary people I've met, and it's really the ordinary people. They don't even have the 'glory' of being under house arrest. One of the things we learned to do in the Communist period was to shine the light on the dissidents, so people would not forget them.

"The issue of witnessing"

"Even Kim Dae Jung, Havel, Mandela, Martin Luther King – people knew about them. And as horrible as it was, they weren't totally alone. Some of these people who trudged the roads in Angola and watched their children having their legs blown off by a mine – people don't know about them. When you put people's faces with that, it really does affect you.

"Different events call for courage, but the actual act is probably the same. The part that strikes me more and more is that ultimately you have no choice but to depend on yourself. I'm a complete extrovert. I love people around me. I get my strength from other people. But in the end you do know that the moment where something is required of you – as you go in and get your mammogram – you are by yourself.

"I find going to get a mammogram takes more courage than almost anything.

"Now we're experiencing this on such a large scale – the issue of the mammogram, dealing with profound uncertainty. I don't think we're genetically programmed to deal with profound uncertainty."

"I think that's right. The testing process, not just medical, but generally, you take an act and then you have to wait to figure out what the result is. If you're a person who likes to have some control over your life, it's that period when you have no control, the uncertainty. Maybe that is what courage is, trying to deal with uncertainty."

"I really began this piece in relation to awe – testimony to what I saw around me in difficult personal times. With 9/11 there seemed something similar, a heightened awareness of what's valuable…"

Secretary Albright, "The question is how long it lasts."

Chuck Close
Artist

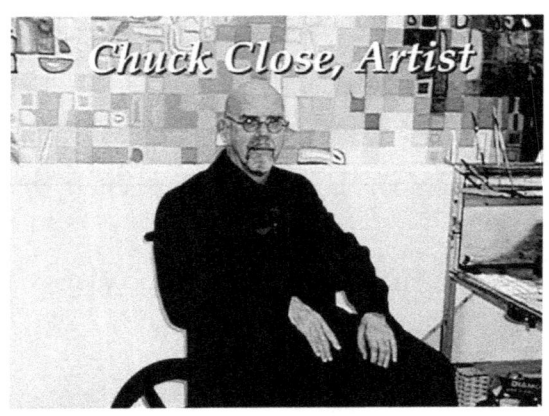

Chuck Close was powerful, calculating and free, aware of himself, thoroughly analyzed, capable of not taking himself too seriously in circumstances that were serious. He was an artist's artist, an artist's friend, a citizen who cared, explored, and knew good Scotch.

I began, "As time has gone on, how I'm come to feel is, it's about life..."

"Yes."

"No matter what else, up until the time when it's not."

Chuck considered, "Yes. My father was very ill most of his life. During my parent's marriage I think four times my mother was told that he was dying, four entirely different diseases or situations. So I grew up with this sense that we're all living on borrowed time. But I also think that I learned that doctors aren't always right. And then finally, the strange gift that – my father did die when I was eleven – the strange gift in his death, it's hard to even talk about anything positive coming out of something like that, but the strange gift was learning very early in life that you can survive tragic circumstances and that you will be happy again.

"Everything that happens to you at some point or other bends or deflects the trajectory of your life. It's just like any-thing else, we're all dealt a hand and some of those hands are shittier hands than others. But it's perfectly possible to win at poker after having been dealt a really bad hand. And it's also possible to lose at poker after having been dealt what should of been a winning hand. So I think it's how you play it. And that's where the pleasure lies.

"I guess a courageous person is somebody who can do something I can't do. Some people have said that since I've been in a wheelchair I exhibit courage, whatever. But it didn't seem to me like I had a whole hell of a lot of choice, and it's so dependent upon my nature. I mean, I am by nature a positive person and that's something I can't take any credit for. I'm just who I am.

"I don't think I've learned anything. I don't think I'm better equipped to handle anything today than I was before. Mine was a brush with death, and then pretty soon it became clear that I was going to survive.

"I may be in denial in that but I must say that I actually forget that I'm in a wheelchair until I roll by a full-length mirror and I'm shocked to see myself like that. But I would say that the reason I feel that way is that I sit as I always sit and I look out at a world which is essentially unchanged, whereas the people around me see me and see what happened. So it's like a fresh wound everyday for them.

"You know, what I do now, if anything, in my re-prioritized existence probably means more to me than it ever did."

"Like once you've give up worrying about things – you've hit the wall".

Chuck parries, "You think you've given up worrying about things?"

"No, actually. But there's a certain part that sees you're at the end of the tunnel – all right, that's where it is."

"Yeah"

"The end game."

Chuck, "Right. You know why New Yorkers are so depressed?"

"No."

"Cause the light at the end of the tunnel is New Jersey."

Susanna Agnelli
First Woman Minister of Foreign Affairs in Italy.
Philanthropist. Sister of Gianni Agnelli, founder of Fiat.

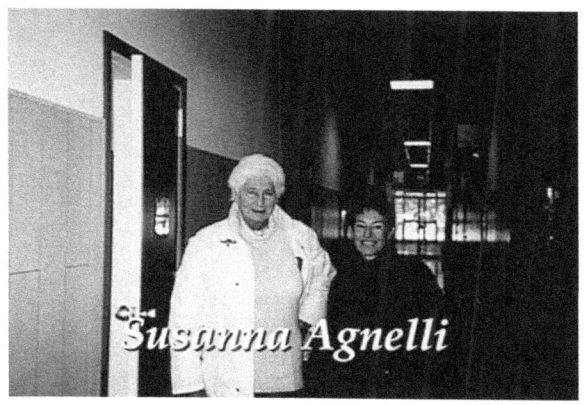

I met Minister Agnelli at the foundation she established in Rome, "Il Faro." (The Lighthouse). It is a school and a refuge for young immigrants recently arrived in Italy. They were often treated badly by the authorities, brought from prison to the foundation, having jumped off boats, trains, etc. to cross the frontier, alone, into Italy.

Here they were taught skills and treated with respect, as individuals who had something to teach, as well as to learn.

"Courage is the greatest sign of liberty there is. To be courageous, one must be free. It is difficult, perhaps impossible to teach courage. Perhaps the only way is to teach by example.

"In government one can't worry about what others think or losing your position. Of course this is a big privilege. Taking a position against public opinion is very difficult."

"Has coming from your family helped or hindered you?"

"As with most things in life, it's 50-50. Fifty percent helps, fifty percent works against me."

"What have been the most courageous things in your life?"

"Crossing the mountains into Switzerland during World War II, certainly. This foundation is a sign of courage. In Italy, immigrants are treated as enemies. Here we are friends.

"To be courageous, you must not listen to the opinions of others, you must be free."

Mike Meyer

Correspondent for Newsweek in the Balkans during the civil war. Communications Director of the U.N. Founding dean of the Graduate School of Media and Communications at Aga Khan University in Nairobi.

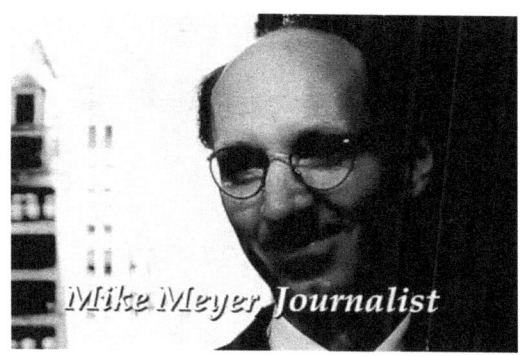

Mike Meyer Journalist

I interviewed Mike Meyer at the New York headquarters of Human Rights Watch, where he happened to be leaning dangrously close to my painting, which hung on a wall of the Board Room. His sensitivity and acute perception of situations around the globe are never predictable, always conveying a deeper insight into the actual causes, influences and ramifications of developing history.

"I remember talking to a woman in Germany who survived World War II. The Americans had just come through and met the Russians down the road. They had a meeting in their jeep, the Russians went one way, the Americans went in another.

"Suddenly a group of renegade Germans, jumped out of the bushes, shooting the Americans, and stole their jeep. This woman came out of her house where the Americans were lying in the street in blood and gathered their blood to make a soup for her child who was starving, and to go through their pockets to salvage anything she could to help her survive.

"You talk to her 30, 40 years later, with her ruddy cheeks, and the quality of bravery is obvious."

Leon de Santillana
Student

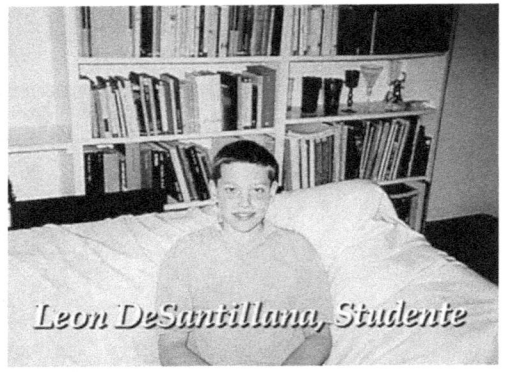

Leon DeSantillana, Studente

Leon is a polite, thoughtful young man. He came in from skipping rocks in the front yard to offer these disturbing comments. It was a time when his parents were divorcing.

"What seems most courageous to do?"

"To have faith in anyone – to have faith. You never know if you can really trust someone."

Four Firemen Speaking Anonymously

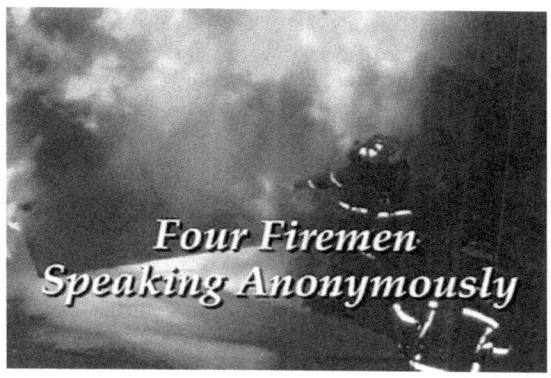

I began this project speaking with these firemen. They were not too interested and were not accustomed to much personal communication with each other. But as we spoke, the subject of courage proved a key into each other, compelling, releasing, for them, for us both, sneaking up on us in its significance. I learned how delicate a thread of communication is from these tough, rock-hard, lovely individuals.

"I think the bigger the fire gets obviously, it's like the bigger the mountain. There's a point where anybody can be overwhelmed by the situation."

"You don't want to put your life in danger. You have to face those judgments on those things."

"You can't look through the walls and see what's going on entirely."

"I mean, you get pumped!"

"Your blood pressure, your heart rate will all be –"

"Elevated."

"Pure beta – flight or fight."

"You sense danger."

"A brush fire is probably in some ways more impressive of the danger of the whole thing. It looks like war – the grandiose picture of this marching wall of smoke and fire and people trying to –"

"Save houses. Or people trying to get out of the way. It's like the plague is coming."

"It's a huge storm. You're caught...It's everywhere. Not one focused spot like a house..."

"It's the whole mountain range."

"The world is on fire."

"The world is on fire."

Spalding Gray
Writer, Actor

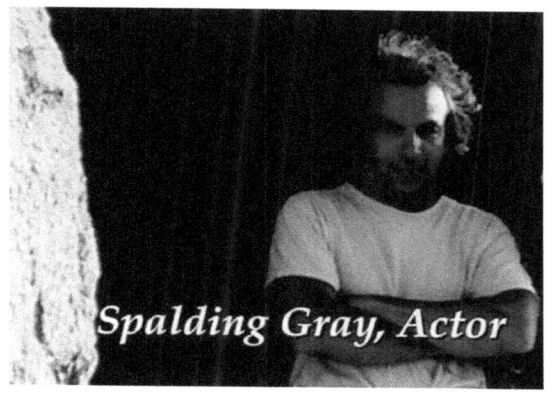

Spalding Gray, Actor

Spalding was a wonderful, complicated person. Flying with Spalding was something never to be recommended. He pointed out emphatically each mountain you were definitely too close to.

"I'd always thought courage would be this pejorative state, this negative state, where you were up against a wall and you say, 'Now my hackles are up, either I lose it and collapse or die, or go cuckoo, or I make a stand.'

"I mean, I have people that I have in my mind that I feel are courageous people. And I bring them up, you know, to give myself inspiration and fortitude.

'Liddy,* I have a vision of her often and her presence and her demeanor in the face of those things that I know about her, things that I've never discussed with her. And she becomes like a force in my life.

The way other people worship God, I think of people, they're human beings that have courage in this world, and they become like a guiding light."

*Liddy was an old friend.

Attilio Codognato
Jeweler, Collector

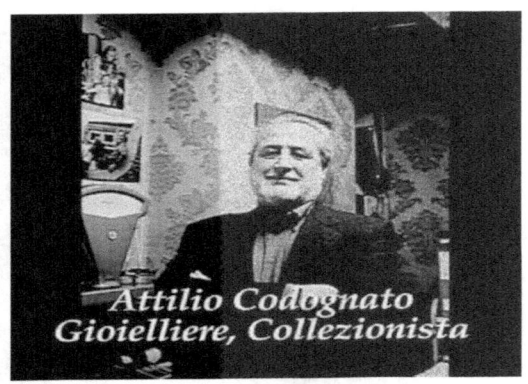

The Codognato family have been the jewelers to the aristocracy of Venice and beyond since 1866. Attilio seems the doge of Venice of our times. A deeply cultured man of profound thought and character. He makes and shows jewelry of time-eclipsing value.

He is unique, in his exquisite golden cabinet of wonders just off the piazza.

"Who brandishes the paintbrush against an empty canvas, measuring himself against nothing, seems enormously courageous. There is all to cover and all to discover. Nothing is there. The canvas is a mirror. We all fear seeing ourselves in a mirror."

President Bill Clinton

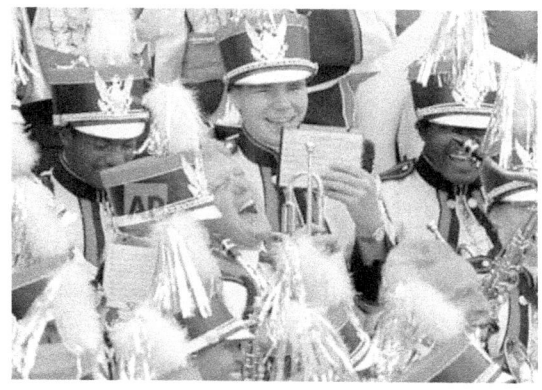

I find this interview particularly poignant, as, in these worst of his days in the White House, President Clinton speaks to himself, exhausted, his spoon clinks to his coffee cup. He thinks razor sharp, clearly, continually, profoundly, alone.

"What do you think courage is?"

"Hemingway said courage is 'grace under pressure.' For me, courage is doing the right thing in difficult circumstances, showing bravery in the face of combat, contests, persisting in the face of abuse, attack or defeat, handling illness or loss with dignity; sometimes just living day to day with a generous spirit in the face of all the problems life presents. Courage is doing what it takes to change, when change is required. Courage is also required to forgive, when you have been wronged or have suffered; trying to live under any given set of circumstances, no matter how difficult, according to what you believe is right and human."

"What do you draw on for this capacity?"

"My religious faith, the power of example from brave people, the encouragement of people of good will, the desire to see the course in which I believe prevail."

"Does courage include fear?"

"Absolutely."

"Doubt?"

"Of course."

"Challenge?"

"Always. The thing that makes courage 'courage' is the fact that there is, underneath it, fear, doubt, challenge. That's why my favorite movie is High Noon. Gary Cooper is scared to death, but he does the right thing anyway."

"Where do you find the greatest examples of courage in history, politics and life?"

"There are lots of examples. Mandela had great courage, first in surviving his 27 years in prison and then in forgiving. My mother showed great courage in the way she handled her final illness, as so many people do.

"In politics, the people who served with me, who had the courage to vote to get rid of our deficit even though it put their political careers at risk, or to take the first steps for gun safety, even though the NRA took a lot of them out of public life, a life they loved very much, those people showed courage."

"How do we find courage in our complicated world?"

"Courage is all around us. It's a great mistake to believe that our almost professional and carefully cultivated cynicism can erase the courage that is there everyday. The courage of parents who have children with physical or mental disabilities, who are determined to love them anyway and raise them to be as much as they can be; the courage of a man like Christopher Reeves, who suffered enormous physical injury and is determined not to give into it, but to overcome it; the courage of combatants in civil, religious, ethnic or tribal wars who find some way to go on and reach out to those they once fought in a spirit of forgiveness.

"Courage is everywhere. It takes courage just to make it through day-to-day life, to meet basic responsibilities, when difficulties arise.

"I think it is a great mistake to believe that because we're not involved in World War II, because we all can't be great athletes, or involved in some other grand contest, that there is a shortage of courage in the world. There is no shortage of courage in the world, most of it displayed everyday by ordinary people dealing with the challenges life presents them, relying on their religious faith, their heart, their instincts and the support of people of good will."

John Podesta
Former Clinton White House Chief of Staff. Hillary Clinton Campaign Chairman 2016. Advisor to President Barak Obama. Founder and Chair of the Center For American Progress.

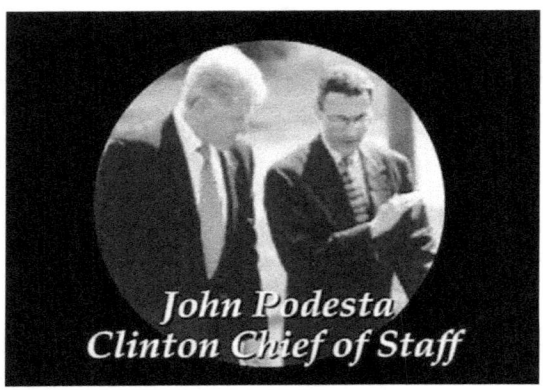

John Podesta has the attributes of a seer, a scholar, an excavator of the truth and salient point, and a comedian – all qualities for success in high echelons of power. And he's a great cook, as history has revealed. His help in this project has been invaluable. I'm proud to be in his hacked emails.

"What do you draw on to meet the challenges in the White House?"

"You have to think that what you're doing is the right thing, you're sort of open to being self-critical while believing that the general thrust where you're going is the right direction. And thinking that the people who are trying to take you in a different direction are generally wrong and worth fighting with. We have the good fortune of picking good enemies."

"Do you see President Clinton as a courageous person?"

"Yes, I think he has pursued his vision of where America can go, and where the world can be, with great vigor. With the force of having made his own personal stands, but also with the force of great antagonism from his political opponents. He's one of the only people I've ever met who could, in the face of all that, get up every day and come to work with a smile on his face and think about what he can do today to make the world a little bit better."

"What does he draw from to be able to do that."

"This must be true of most great presidents, maybe Lincoln would be a counter example. He just has an enormous sense of optimism. In that sense, he embodies the American spirit of 'tomorrow's always going to be better than yesterday.' I think probably most great presidents have had that quality about them, that they're always reaching for a little bit more, they're always optimistic about where the future is. That kind of defines, I think, the American character."

Luigi Sfrizo
Fish Vendor

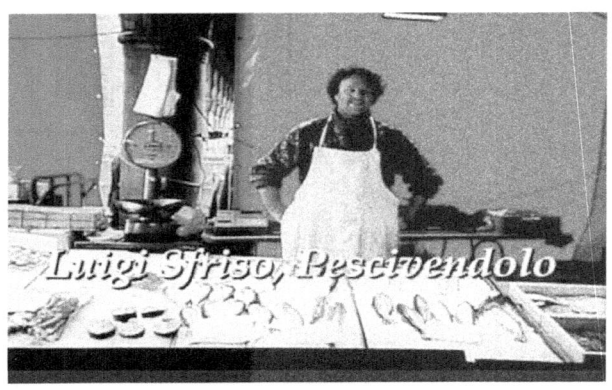

This man always looked like he was enjoying his day. He had excellent fish, frequently dispalyed a bit oddly.

"Courage!   I thought you were going to ask me about fish!"

Former Italian Prime Minister Silvio Berlusconi

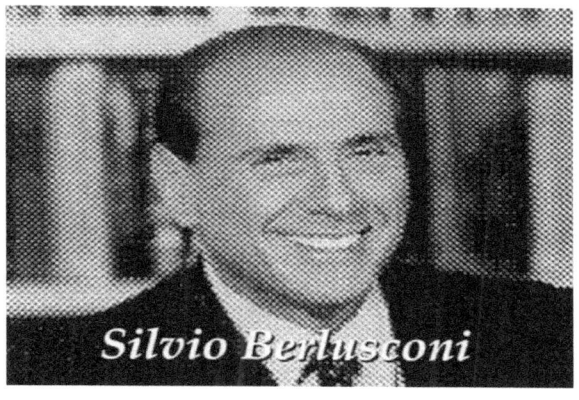

Silvio Berlusconi

In the flickering light of the Temple of Hadrian, I wondered, "What was that?" The piazza's resident guitarist, a prodigy from Albania, strummed for coins at his post by a towering column, symbol of a great power that once was. Two hours with Italy's Prime Minister led one right into thoughts on time, space, history and relative perceptions of reality – fueled by a couple shots of the best espresso in Rome.

The saga of my conversation with Silvio Berlusconi began when the curator of the Venice Biennale, Harald Szeemann, where I was preparing to exhibit this project, and I were talking about prominent Europeans and this elusive investigation into courage. The Pope would be good, he thought, Milosevic on the dark side, and why not give a try for Berlusconi. My inclination ran towards the fish vendor, gondolieri, Susanna Agnelli ... but why not?

I thoroughly expected a secretary with blonde helmet hair and an attitude towards me of artist-equals-tax-liability, quite the contrary here. I've always thought you could tell a lot about a country by who they name their bars for and in Italy it's for artists. I met the young Smith graduate, assistant to Berlusconi, who after much back and forth and "absolutely impossibles" suggested I submit my questions and they'd think about it.

45

This is the only instance in which I've been asked to submit the questions beforehand.

My Italian is particularly good when it comes to gelato but I amped it up with considerable assistance from the staff of the American Academy in Rome. We secured a date at the discreetly but much guarded Prime Minister's office in the center of Rome, just around the corner from the Temple of Hadrian.

I walked through the bustling, crumbling streets of Trastevere through the Piazza Navonna with Bernini's sculptures of tension and beauty urging me on. I practiced my questions on the clerk in the local hardware store. Her answers were interesting, helped me get my pacing down and hone what to listen for. Of course she was from a small town near Calabria, keen to sell me this great ground glass pigment no one had inquired about for years and was not the Prime Minister. Nonetheless, with a little Campari and her blessings I walked around the corner to the Prime Minister's palazzo and gave my name to the well-dressed security.

It's a great palazzo. I would have paid just for the frescoes and the smell. That smell which is perhaps why we travel – age, intrigue, time transport, some kind of permeation of the pores by an 'other'.

They left me in a reception hall. Heavy power in dark suits came and went, but I was in fact having fun, and not too nervous. It was such a performance and I love a good performance. I was on my second cappuccino, which the guard/escort assured me was the best in Rome and I should also have please a biscotti or maybe a sandwich, when the pony-tailed "assistant" with whom I'd by then had considerable contact, arrived to accompany me into our meeting.

She seemed fairly nervous. The walls of the office are covered with significant tapestries in an elegant, thoroughly considered context for the emergence of the bustling prime minister.

We looked pretty well eye to eye and he had that tan of those who enjoy their position of well being. He couldn't have been more gracious, offering another coffee while railing against the press and prosecutors and why do they continually hound him. This was during the height of one of the many investigations into his business practices and why should they be picking on him? I actually understood quite well, but asked about the tapestries.

As we sat down the assistant said she had typed out my questions and gave me the pages. This threw me entirely as the language was different from my well rehearsed cadences at the hardware store. But okay, I could do it. There seemed to be a corresponding paper discreetly on his desk. He asked me if I wanted to do an equipment check and was somewhat disconcerted when I said no. My goal is to get responses as immediate as possible. In fact I'd already done a test with my extremely simple tape recorder while they were milling about.

I asked, "What is courage to you?"

He looked directly at me, "The willingness to risk yourself, what you are, what you have, up to the very end for what you love. Ultimately it is an act of love."

I've had many conversations on this subject and not heard this thought, and I was never to hear it again. I was also curious as to who penned the responses. I asked, "What are the greatest examples of courage that you've seen in your life?

Berlusconi paused and answered, "I've known from close up the courage of my mother during the German occupation when she physically opposed the SS to keep one of her friends from being deported. She was put against a wall and risked being shot. At the last minute she was saved, by a miracle."

I asked what the miracle was but the assistant said that was not in my questions. My next question, "What for you are the greatest examples of courage in history?"

He continued, "It is difficult, perhaps improper to make a hierarchy. But I certainly know and am moved by the stories of men and women exposed to the arbitrary influences of power. I have seen the terrible physical and psychological damage they have suffered for faith in their beliefs and ideals, defending their dignity and liberty. These stories show the greatness that man can be."

I was struck by how quiet the office was. No one in or out, no phones ringing, machines churning and the true miracle: no ringing of cellulare. It was the office of a patrician at well-designed work, at least in the front office.

To my next question, "Do you feel physical courage is different from the courage it takes to make difficult political decisions?" he answered, "Sometimes it also takes physical courage in politics, knowing you are accepting a great and serious risk to your health and even your life. In some ways politics is truly an extreme sport."

I knew he had some experience with cancer and asked if that had affected his perspective on governance. We spoke a bit about the surprising effects of difficult circumstances. Yes, he had been affected.

To my next question, "What have been your major moments of courage?" he responded, "The work of a businessman that I have done in my life has made me accustomed to risk, it has become a normal dimension for me. But nothing comparable to my decision to enter politics. At my age where rightly I could enjoy the fruits of my life's work, I entered a new risky adventure. Rather than enjoy my tranquility and not become involved with my country, which runs the risk of grave danger, I chose to not ignore the call of the majority of Italians needing to fight a small untruthful minority who would make a suffocating and illiberal future.

"For this I have risked everything, knowing I would find myself against a potent establishment in a heavy campaign of hate. I would be assaulted by the legal system while my family would have to make sacrifices as well.

"I don't know if this merits the name courage. When I think about it, it seems crazy. But the kind of crazi- ness that makes life noble. In the story of mankind, salvation some- times depends on the craziness of a few brave people. In my case, that of deciding to proceed as I have, I remember what Erasmus of Rotterdam wrote, 'The most just decision, the most wise decision, is not that which comes from the brain, but that which comes from farsighted, visionary imagination.'"

To my last question, "From what do you draw courage?" Berlusconi answered, "From those who wish me well, from my faith, from the encouragement of the people I am fortunate to have around me, from the thoughts of many others, from the faith that many have put in me."

We spoke for some time afterwards. The Prime Minis- ter was affable and generous, finding our considerations a respite from his usual afternoons. We took photos. Actually sorry it was over, I found my way back into the fading twilight of the piazza fronting the Temple of Hadrian, in its glory, mag- nificence, intelligence and folly that was Rome.

Gondolieri

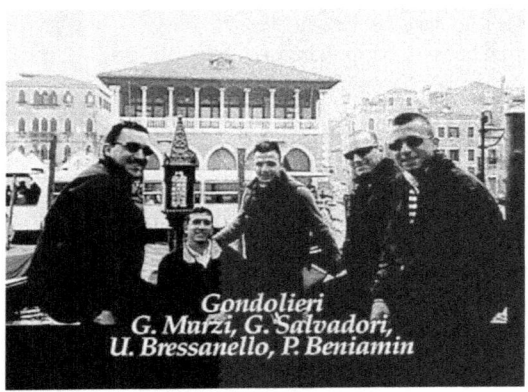

Gondolieri
G. Marzi, G. Salvadori,
U. Bressanello, P. Beniamin

These gondolieri didn't sing and seemed to pay a good deal of attention to the weather, while always being up for a laugh.

"Are gondolieri couragous?"

"It's not courage we have - we're masochists! Actually, it's the tourists who are courageous going with us. They don't know what the situation is.

"Fear is everywhere, courage is hidden. It's in your DNA. It's the force that moves some people and blocks others."

Gen. Norman Schwarzkopf

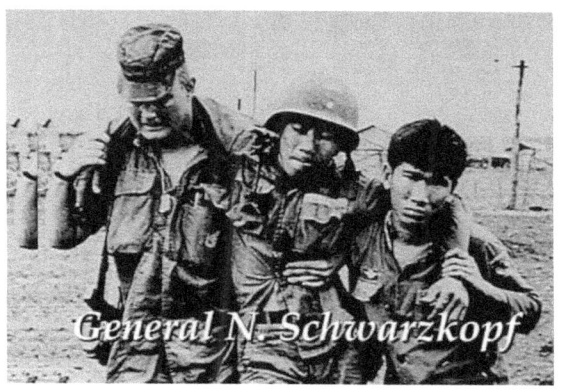

General Schwarzkopf was a complete surprise. Here was someone I imagine many had quite justifiably feared. Finding Gen. Schwarzkopf was not easy. The Pentagon doesn't talk, he was not listed in the phone book. He was involved in serious philanthropy.

I had wanted to speak with someone who would embody a certain kind of archetype. In fact, Gen. Schwarzkopf was entirely specific, nobody's archetype. It was easy to imagine him in a general's uniform. He was wearing a semi-Hawaiian shirt. Same man, deeply rooted beyond the outfit.

Once I found him in his Tampa office, he listened to what I was up to and immediately agreed to see me. No submitting of questions, security check or limiting of access. I was on my own - and so was he. From the very first call, it was clear that he listened. And what I do is listen, for the words, for the spaces in between the words, for the tone of what they're composed and how it rolls back and forth, never predictable, revolving back, hanging off the edge.

The General was, to a New York artist, quite a curiosity. He was the only person I traveled to see, at the height of hurricane season, and I don't like to fly. So I reserved a convertible and made a reservation where the moss draped most.

It was 98% humidity as I arrived and parked across from a Cuban cigar store. Gen. Schwarzkopf's office was in the best-looking building downtown -- on the same street as an excellent used book store, where I got him a large book, literature as shield.

His name was not on the building's roster. The lobby smelled like roasting chicken. An attendant sent me to an office covered with photos of Gen. Schwarzkopf with groups of children and a lot of pictures of dogs with assorted birds in their mouths. There was nothing to do with war anywhere.

The General was strong. He shook your hand and you knew it. I liked him immediately. He was straightforward, educated in Switzerland, from a family that took him all over world. He told me a story of how, as a child, he was once the guest of honor with his father in a tent in the desert as the nomad chieftain offered him their prized delicacy, a sheep's eye. I didn't have much of a comeback, although I was once offered a bull's ear in a bullring in Spain with Salvador Dali. Apparently I did not do much better with the ear than the General did with the eyeball.

He was interested in talking about courage. In reading his autobiography, I had been affected by the letter he wrote to his wife as he was going into war. I said I thought it was not only beautiful, but to be able to say that you weren't afraid to die. How do you come to a point to feel that?

He answered, "You know what Shakespeare said in Julius Caesar? 'Cowards die many times before their death. The valiant never taste of death but once. Of all the wonders I yet have heard, it seems to me most strange that men should fear, seeing that death, a necessary end, will come when it will come.' That's sort of fatalistic. I don't want to die. I want to be immortal.

"I mean, if you've been in battle, it's so interesting how the difference between life and death is mere fractions. When I was wounded the first time in Vietnam, this fellow opened up on me, it was obvious that he had shot at me with an automatic weapon. And it was obvious that his sights were not adjusted properly, because I was standing in an armored vehicle and my body was sticking way out.

The Vietnamese had piled boxes all over the floor as they were short, it was the only way they could see out – so they were looking out with their heads and I was way up out of the tank. The bullet marks went, boom, boom, boom, boom, right up the side of the armed personnel carrier, right where I was standing. I mean, absolutely, I was standing there with my arm ... they went boom, boom, boom, you can see, like that."

And he showed me.

"I got hit in the arm," he continued, "And I guess the splatter got me in the face. But if that fellow had had one more click of elevation on his sights, he would have cut me in half, killed me. Quite literally it was a question of fractions."

This was a big man to be measuring fractions. He knew where he was standing and was not interested in towing the party line, any party line.

"Right now I'm waging a major battle against the U.S. Government for more funding for cancer for crying out loud. I have sort of a thematic that goes, we spent $60 million to overthrow, to get Saddam Hussein and kick him out of Kuwait – and it was money well spent. We saved thousands of lives by spending that $60 million." This conversation was in relation to the Gulf War.

"But how much do you think we would spend if we found out that Saddam Hussein suddenly had a secret weapon, and that secret weapon was going to kill 1,500 every single day. And it was going to end up wounding one out of every two men and one out of every three women? How much money would we spend to destroy that, if we spent $60 million to get him back into Iraq? How much would we spend if he had this kind of weapon? Yet, that's exactly what cancer does. Cancer kills 1,500 people every day. Cancer kills more people every two days than were killed in Pearl Harbor.

"And yet, last year the government spent $2.2 billion in cancer research. You know how much one B-2 bomber costs? $2.2 billion. Now, that's disgraceful."

He got up and paced around the room, showing me some of the material from a camp for children with cancer that he funded with Paul Newman, among others. They all looked like warriors. I brought up the subject of war.

"I don't equate courage with war. I think everyday there are people who are making very courageous decisions about their own personal health, about the health of their family, about the future of their family ... You know, I certainly didn't volunteer to have cancer ...

"I like life. There was my life before I found out I had cancer, and then there was life after I found out I had cancer."

I asked, "Do you think you live differently when you deal with life with a degree of uncertainty?"

He paused, his only pause in our entire hour's conversation, "Well, life is uncertain."

"Yes ... how do you deal with fear? Even fear, I think, is fear part of courage?"

"Fear is good. There's nothing wrong with fear. I think fear sharpens your senses. It helps you to be smart, to remember your training. I mean, you're trained to survive. You're not trained to die. You're trained to survive. Fear sharpens all of our senses. There's nothing wrong with fear. It's how your body prepares itself for whatever it is you're going to go through, and it helps you. It's only when fear becomes so overwhelming that it paralyzes you, that it paralyzes you from action, that it becomes bad.

"Then I guess that fear is really no longer fear, it's terror. The only thing we have to fear is fear itself, right? I mean, there's nothing wrong with being scared. I talk to young kids, underprivileged children, and one of the questions they always ask me is, 'Weren't you afraid?' And I say, 'Sure. Because there's nothing wrong with being afraid.'

"The only time I've ever really been frightened – really, really frightened – was in this mine field. I was standing here and this young kid was laying over there, and I knew we were in the middle of a mine field and nobody else was going to walk over there and help that kid.

"I was the battalion commander, it was my job to do that, knowing that I had to walk from here to there, where any given step would've blown my leg off, or blown my head off. I was scared. I mean, it was the only time my knees have ever shaken. Literally, when I'd take a step, my knees would shake so that I had to hold the knee. And I'd take the next step. I clearly understood that the outcome could be very unfavorable.

"It's interesting, unit cohesion is an important thing in battle. When you ask yourself, 'What is it that makes the Marine continue up the hill in the face of overwhelming machine gun fire raining down on him? What is it that makes a soldier stay in a foxhole when he looks down on the valley and there are 10,000 screaming Chinese running across the valley at him?

"Study after study has shown that the single most important thing is unit cohesion. They will not get up and run away, not because of God, Country and Mom's apple pie, but because they don't want to let down their buddy on their left and their right."

I wondered if he felt there was a difference between bravery and courage, something I had been thinking about and at least partially expected West Point to come through here.

He answered, "An act of valor is not necessarily an act of courage. True courage to me is when someone clearly recognizes that what they are about to do could have dire consequences. But because their moral strength, their moral belief, their moral courage is so strong, they understand that they must do it despite the consequences. That to me is true courage."

So no West Point. No following of orders, less value for the instinctive act though it proves valorous.

In conclusion I asked, "If you could choose an example of courage that you've seen what might it be?"

His answer, "Gee, there're so many. I mean, nothing's coming -- actually everything is coming to me. I'm into sensory overload ... the Bataan Death March. There were countless acts of courage where people, in order to save their buddies, placed themselves in huge danger... tunnel rats in Vietnam, they used to go down into the tunnels – climb down in the tunnels with a flashlight and a .45 pistol, knowing that was not a good place to be. Then go through these tunnels, many times encountering, not the enemy, but snakes in there, and that sort of thing. You never would have gotten me down one of those holes, I tell you that right now!" (Laughing)

Othello Ghigi
Electrician

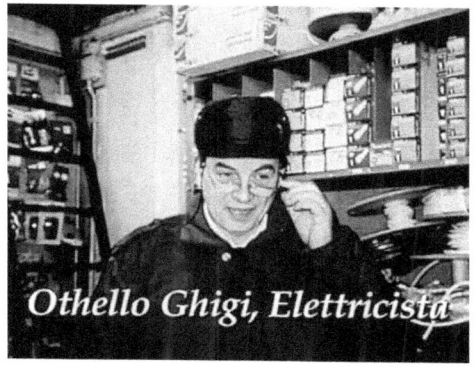

The electrician's store was the defacto community center of an outlying Venetian neighborhood, because he was so smart; and the pet store, with an enormous cardboard dog on its roof, was next door.

"I've seen people here kicked out of their houses, sometimes old, sick, they face a challenge, a very difficult challenge, and they figure it out. When a big challenge happens and one is able to maintain an equilibrium, a harmony with life, that's courage. To begin again from nothing.

"Throwing yourself out of a plane with a parachute is not courage, it's exhibitionism or trying to show you're superior.

A heroic gesture is a gesture of vanity."

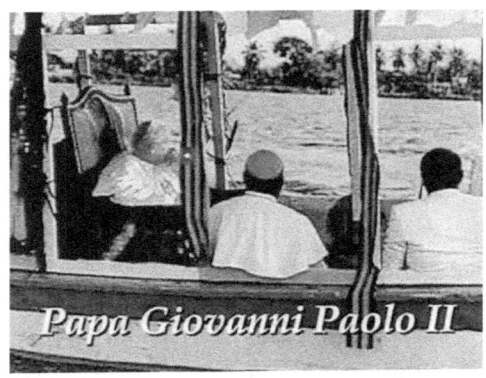

Papa Giovanni Paolo II

I never expected to speak to the Pope, but the journey of the attempt brought myriad unexpected insights into belief, bureaucracy and spectacle. The Pope's comments here come from his address to the new Cardinals, which I was invited to attend, sitting close to the front, watching the engaged, enraptured faces of many of the new Cardinals as they entered into this marriage with the Church.

Entering St. Peter's Square, after being frisked by Vatican security, the Swiss Guard, dressed in their uniforms designed by Michelangelo, I took my seat behind Queen Sofia of Spain.

"Andiamo avanti." Translation: "We go forward. We continue."

Dr. Holly Andersen
Cardiologist

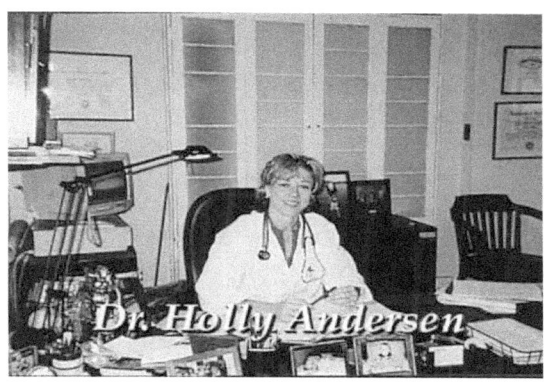

Dr. Andersen personifies what it means to give care – to be a doctor.

In her office filled with diplomas of professional accomplishments, photos of her adorable children and a plastic golfer, she evaluates the most serious of circumstances. She is a warrior, grace under pressure. She thinks everything is possible and looks at everything realistically, assuring her patients that whatever it is, they will find a way through, even if it is a way through to the end.

I came to Dr. Andersen because I couldn't stop coughing. I wanted cough syrup with large amounts of opiates and to be done quickly. In retrospect, I remember her deeply considered resolve as the examination progressed. She was so blonde, so beautiful.

I'd had too many tests when I'd broken my pelvis some time back, the east wall of the MRI room was surely constructed by my contributions. Dr. Andersen scheduled a battery of tests, which I immediately cancelled. She rescheduled.

Dr. Andersen pays attention with her entirety, as well as with her vast knowledge and capacity. This sets her apart. She is *right there in the known and unknown of the phenomena, the gentle integrity of her reactions setting the tone for your own.*

A relationship based on mortality is like no other, in its scale, in its perspective ...

I asked Dr. Andersen, now several years later, to talk with me about courage. I'd never sat in her office in a chair. It was a moment, a privilege, an accomplishment, our accomplishment, perhaps beyond any other.

"There was one gentleman who came in when I was a fellow in cardiology, having a huge heart attack in the emergency room about four in the morning, huge. Back then we were using this clot-busting medicine called TPA. We gave it to him and it started working, but then his heart just stopped, it went all the way down to nothing. So I gave him another medicine to get his heart back, put a pacemaker in him and the pacemaker started working and the medicine started working and he started recovering from his heart attack.

"We brought him into the Intensive Care Unit about six in the morning, and he was pretty stable. His pacemaker was working, his blood pressure was okay, he was awake, his pain was going away, his electrocardiogram was getting better. Right as I watched him, his heart went out. Just right, right there. He's talking to me, he's getting chest pains – he went out.

"I, of course, took him to the ICU. The paddles are right there so I took the paddles, I shocked him, he came back and we put him on the air bag. We're wheeling him into the cath lab where we did an angiogram and opened up his artery and put in this balloon pump, and he recovered.

"He goes into this story, 'I remember being...' He remembers being out at night and then he doesn't remember too much. Then he said, 'I remember floating and I was back in my childhood town and I was on this river and there was this...'

You hear the story, this guy had no idea where he was. 'I saw this big light, and I started going to it, it was very welcoming and I was, I wanted to go, and I wanted to go, but then something kept calling me, somebody kept calling my name, 'Come back.' Somebody, I couldn't go, someone just kept calling me.'

"And it was very interesting, because he didn't know that basically he had experienced sudden death and been brought out of it and came back. 'I really wanted to relax and go, but somebody kept calling me.'

"It was a very interesting story. And I was there when he woke up, so I know no one prepped him as to what happened.

"It was one example of many. I've seen people go peacefully and people fight to come back. As much as we can do, as much as I shocked this guy out of his sudden death and his heart going out, you can't do everything. I mean, I don't take credit for everything and even though it's really hard to lose somebody; I don't, anytime you lose somebody, anytime I lose somebody, over and over and over again, especially someone you didn't expect to lose, you go over things – 'Is there anything else I could have done, what more could we have done?

What did we miss?' You have to realize you're not in control of everything. As much as you want to be, you're not.

"I think courage is the ability to face the truth, to face the truth in yourself, to live the truth in yourself and to explore the truth in yourself.

"And I think to try to live a happy life takes courage, because it's so much easier to complain and be miserable. And people are much more comfortable and secure in, I think, in general – not everybody, but in general – being unhappy, and 'woe is me,' than to take the courage to say, 'I'm happy, I'm going to take this gift of life and make it a celebration.'"

About the Author

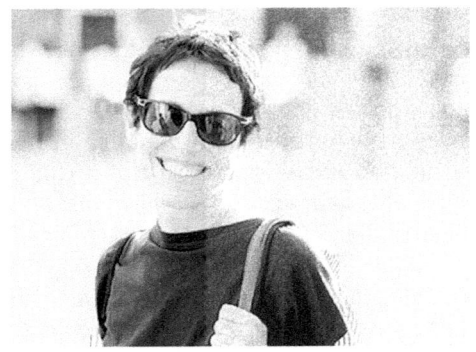

    Susan Kleinberg was a New York-based artist. She had work in four Venice Biennales; PS1/MoMA; Castelli Gallery; Palazzo Fortuny, Venice, in *TRA, PROPORIO and INTUITION;* the Istanbul Biennal; Museum of Fine Arts Buenos Aires, LOOP Barcelona; Total Museum, Seoul, Korea; retrospective at Açikeran Museum, Istanbul; Fondazione Sandretto Re Rebaudengo...

    This piece has been a continuing gift to her.

Editor, Les Guthman

Special Thanks To:

Harald Szeemann
The Venice Biennale
The American Academy in Rome
MoMA PS1
Daniela Ferretti
Manuela Luca Dazio
Axel Vervoordt
John Podesta
Daniel Marzona
Alanna Heiss
Laura de Santillana
Charles Forscher
18th Street Arts Center
Joan Abrahamson
Holly Andersen
George Cyril
Allen Letgolts

Samsung

In Sweet Memory

Susan Kleinberg 1949-2023

Susan passed away peacefully in her studio on December 1, 2023, after a quarter century of beating the odds over a rare cancer, liposarcoma.

She had a storied life in Art, beginning when she was 18, studying Gaudi in Barcelona, and went to a bullfight with Salvador Dali. She graduated from Pomona College, where she studied with Jim Turrell, and got her masters at Hunter, where she studied with Robert Morris and Tony Smith.

Her first loft in New York was on White Street in Tribeca before it was TRIBECA. Only a few years earlier it had been Barnet Newman's studio. Larry Bell and Mel Bochner were her neighbors in the building.

Her first major show in New York was at Leo Castelli's uptown gallery. Her work was in one room, Robert Rauschenberg was in the other. A thrill!

She had a beautiful show one year at the Public Theater on Lafayette St., in the lobby of the theater where Broadway deities Jessica Tandy and Hume Cronin were starring in another of their major theatrical events.

In 1995, for the Venice Biennale's "Arte Laguna," she floated "Spozalizio del Mare" in the Grand Canal between San Marco and San Giorgio. We spent an enchanted week on the island of San Servolo in the Venice Lagoon securing the objects from Venetian history that Susan had made at a Broadway set design studio in Brooklyn, and which she had spray painted gold on the front stoop of her loft at 29 Mercer Street in Soho. (The stoop retained specks of gold paint for a decade later...)

The thousand-year-old Venetian ceremony, Spozalizio del Mare, symbolized the marriage of the Venetian Republic with the sea. On Ascension Day, the Doge threw a gold ring into the Grand

Canal, or into the Adriatic. Susan's gold ring was created by the guys who had made the yellow floatation collars for the Apollo spacecraft.

When we were finished fastening all of the objects onto the trampoline-like inner layer of the "ring" and tried with two-dozen strong arms to lift it, Susan worried that it was too heavy and would sink. She called the guys, still in Cape Canaveral, although the technology was now used for oil spill barriers, They said, "Susan, don't worry, you could float a Chevrolet on it!" We dropped it in the lagoon, it floated perfectly and was towed out into the Grand Canal, where divers dropped the

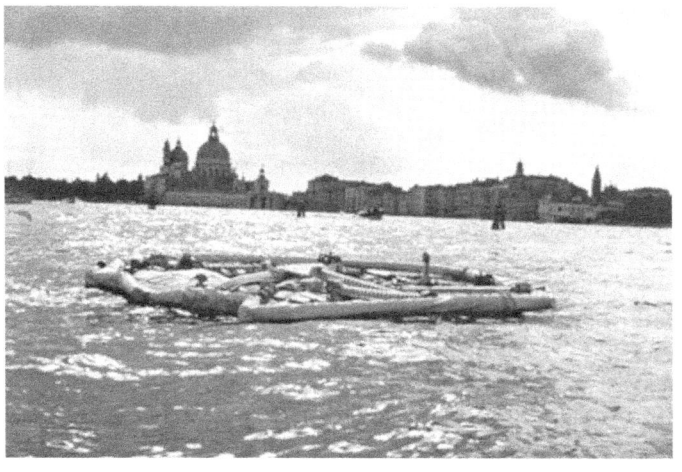

In 1997, Susan was at the American Academy in Rome after having her first major cancer surgery. She had been deeply moved by the courage she saw among other cancer patients and began working on her piece, "Fear Not," in which she asked people of all walks of life what courage meant to them. Everyone from Gore Vidal, whom she visited at his villa in Ravello on the Amalfi Coast and sat in his "Ben Hur" chairs, to a Dominican domestic worker on the Upper West Side in Manhattan. Besides Vidal, her favorite interviews in English were with Astronaut Sally Ride and Congressman and Civil Rights legend John Lewis.

In 2000, Harold Szeemann, who was curating the 2001 Venice Biennale, invited her to show "Fear Not" in the Arsenale. But he asked her to do an Italian version along with the English version. Susan spoke Italian well and spent the year doing just that. She asked the two candidates for prime minister of Italy for interviews. Only Silvio Berlusconi said "yes." Her favorite Italian interviews were with philanthropist Susanna Agnelli, a fish vender in the Rialto market and with three gondolieri. The fish vendor first exclaimed, "Courage? I thought you wanted to talk about fish!"

In the middle of the Arsenale, Susan created a beautiful space with iridescent walls a color somewhere between deep blue and purple. Samsung gave her cutting-edge jewel-like video monitors, which were new and rare at that time. Sennheiser donated elegant black headphones that swayed in the air, hanging down in the high Arsenale ceiling.

For the 2005 Biennale, with sponsorship from the Istituto Veneto di Scienze, Lettere ed Arti in Venice, she projected her video piece "Blood Roll" across the Campo Santo Stefano onto the institute's high white facade. The low rumble of the digital glass globe filled with blood rolling up and down and spinning on a central fulcrum could be heard far outside the Campo...

In 2009, with sponsorship from Telecom Italia, she previewed her second video installation, "Tierra Sin Males," projecting it

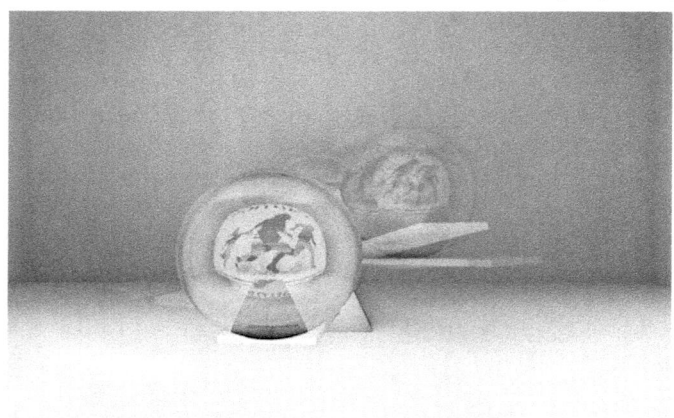

across the broad inner courtyard of the 16th Century Cloister of San Salvador designed by Sansovino.

"Tierra Sin Males" had its formal premiere at the 2011 Venice Biennale in Axel Vervoordt and Daniella Ferretti's first of four renowned Biennale exhibitions at the Palazzo Fortuny, TRA. The following year, the 3D version of "Tierra Sin Males" premiered at Art Basel Miami.

Susan's third video installation, "KAIROS," premiered in Vervoordt and Ferretti's third Palazzo Fortuny show, PROPORTIO, for the 2015 Biennale.

And her fourth, "BALAFRE," premiered in their final Palazzo Fortuny exhibition, INTUITION, for the 2017 Biennale. Both "KAIROS" and "BALAFRE" evolved out of Susan's six-year collaboration with the scientific team at the Louvre in Paris, using their high-resolution HI-Rox digital microscope.

Susan returned to the Louvre in 2017 and created her video installation "HELIX," which premiered at the Antonio Pasqualino International Puppet Museum in Palermo, Italy, a UNESCO World Heritage Site, coinciding with Manifesta 18.

LEAP!

LEAP! was an exquisite leap of faith at a very dark time for her in 2020. She had woken up from her fifth cancer surgery with her right leg paralyzed. The surgeon at Cedars Sinai Hospital in Los Angeles had unknowingly severed the femoral nerve in her leg. And COVID was raging. She began intense physical therapy, although she was told she would never walk again without a walker. (She did, thanks to a surgeon she happened to hear about a year later, who connected two minor nerves in her thigh to the dead femoral nerve and brought it back to life!)

We went to Venice in October 2022, where she did what she never thought she would be able to do again, to walk up and down the canal bridges on her own – to be able to walk around her beloved Venice. And she attended the fabulous three-day conference organized by Simone Leigh, the American artist in the 2022 Biennale (who had transformed the American Pavilion into an African hut...).

Not long after her 2020 surgery, Susan was enamored of a viral video of dolphins returning to the Grand Canal, reportedly because of the clean waters from the COVID collapse of tourism in Venice. She loved the video even if it were false. It turned out to have been shot in Sardinia, but Susan began a series of related drawings and created a video with images of dolphins in Venice. She was in love with the idea, the cleansing and renewal.

"LEAP is an offer of a moment of wonder," she said. As our dear friend Maria Morris Hambourg wrote, "It radiates Susan's creative joy, love of the world, and generosity of feeling." A year later, two dolphins did return to the Grand Canal.

— Les Guthman

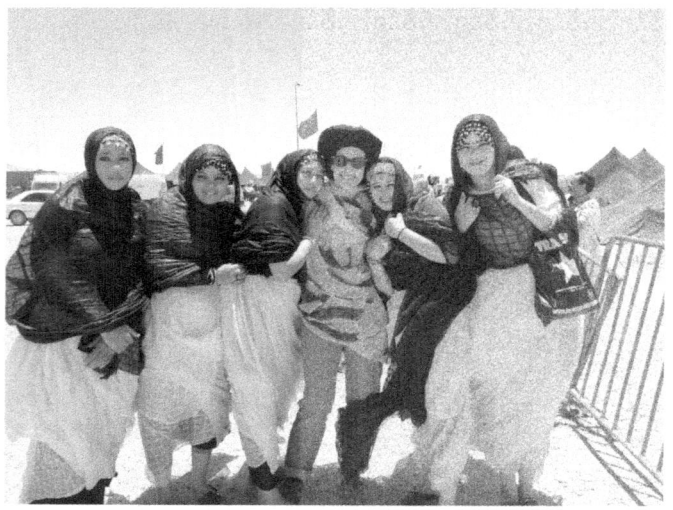

With Berber girls, Moussem de Tan Tan, Morocco, 2014

www.ingramcontent.com/pod-product-compliance
Lightning Source LLC
Chambersburg PA
CBHW061205180526
45170CB00002B/967